Comprehension Mini-Lessons

Sequencing and Context Clues

by LeAnn Nickelsen
with Sarah Glasscock

NEW YORK • TORONTO • LONDON • AUCKLAND • SYDNEY
MEXICO CITY • NEW DELHI • HONG KONG • BUENOS AIRES

SCHOLASTIC
Teaching
Resources

I would like to thank the following people for this book:

my husband, Joel, and my twin children, Keaton and Aubrey, for encouraging and supporting me with the goal of writing this book.

my parents, Jim and Dolores Heim, for helping me with ideas and for all their support. Thanks Mom and Dad for creating the "Who Am I?" activity.

Virginia Dooley, my senior editor, for helping me become a more concise writer and for all of the writing opportunities she has given me.

Sarah Glasscock, my cowriter, and Sarah Longhi, my editor, who spent numerous hours checking over this book to make sure it was perfect.

Katie Lucarelle for her work on student samples.

my sister, Sherry DeVilbiss, for being a great, supportive friend. I know you really wanted your name to be in a book, so here it is (hahaha).

my education friends who have taught with me through the years. You know so much and have contributed so much time and effort. You know who you are!

Grapevine-Colleyville ISD in Texas for supplying me with resources and advice. Anne Simpson, your knowledge is valued by many. Thanks for the help with summarization and main idea.

—LeAnn Nickelsen

Cover design by Norma Ortiz

Cover art by Jason Robinson

Interior design by Sydney Wright

Interior illustrations by Teresa Southwell

Stationery illustration page 26 by Kristen Kest

ISBN 0-439-43833-0

Printed in the U.S.A.

1 2 3 4 5 6 7 8 9 10 40 09 08 07 06 05 04

Contents

Introduction

The *Comprehension Mini-Lessons* Series

National and state standards, and schools across the country require all students to master a set of reading objectives, with an emphasis on these key comprehension areas: main idea, summarizing, inference, cause and effect, point of view, fact and opinion, sequencing, and context clues. For me and the teachers I work with, teaching students to deepen their comprehension has always required several creative lessons for each reading objective to ensure that everyone achieves success. Customizing each lesson plan is a lot of work, and that's where this series of high-interest mini-lessons—the product of years of classroom lesson successes—comes to the rescue.

Each book in this series provides you with several different mini-lessons for each objective, which appeal to different learning styles and help you reach each and every learner. The mini-lessons include activities and real-world examples, so that students have fun learning the reading objective and find the skills they learn useful in their everyday reading and pertinent to their lives.

About This Book

This book presents lessons that teach students skills and strategies for understanding sequencing and context clues.

Sequencing

The brain seeks meaning from what it already knows. This is why knowing the order of events in a text is crucial to understanding the whole story and predicting what will happen next. Time-order words such as first, second, next, and so on, lead a reader to visualize the order of and relationship among events and serve as clues to understanding the events within a time frame. Readers who build skills in sequencing can visualize what is happening, make sense of the story line, predict what may happen based on the time and order of events in a story, and better understand the causes and effects of events.

Context Clues

Writers often suggest the meanings of words that may be unfamiliar to their readers through words or hints that surround the word. Understanding how to seek out clues in the context of the passage to determine the meaning of unknown words allows readers to continue without having to stop and disrupt the flow of reading, helps readers gain a deeper understanding of the whole passage, and increases accuracy in predicting word meanings.

How to Use This Book

You'll find five mini-lessons on sequencing and five on context clues with activities that stimulate different learning styles. I recommend teaching the lessons sequentially. The first lesson introduces the objective in simple terms. The subsequent lessons elaborate on the objective and offer students different skills to better understand it. The last lesson features the objective in a standardized test format, which helps familiarize students with the test language and structure.

A final project pulls the whole concept together and offers students an opportunity to demonstrate creatively what they learned in the mini-lessons. Students also get to share their learning with other classmates when they complete a project. Whenever students teach other students what they have learned, the learning becomes more cemented in their brains.

Notice that each lesson contains anticipatory sets, which enable you to grab students' attention when you open the lesson, and special closures to end the lesson so that students' brains can have another opportunity to absorb the learning. Also included are activities that you can send home to extend the learning in another real-world setting.

—*LeAnn Nickelsen*

Young Adult Fiction Resources

Here are some suggestions for young adult titles that support the objectives in this book:

Books That Support Sequencing

Carrick, Carol. *Aladdin and the Wonderful Lamp*. New York: Scholastic, 1989.

Christian, Mary B. *Nothing Much Happened Today*. Reading, MA: Addison-Wesley, 1973.

Dahl, Roald. *James and the Giant Peach*. New York: Puffin Books, 1961.

Goble, Paul. *The Girl Who Loved Wild Horses*. New York: Bradbury Press, 1978.

Books With Rich Vocabulary Supported by Context Clues

Avi. *Poppy*. London: Watts Publishing/Orchard Books, 1995.

Creech, Sharon. *Walk Two Moons*. New York: Scholastic, 1994.

Curtis, Christopher Paul. *Bud, Not Buddy*. Random House, 1999.

Gross, Virginia T. *The Day It Rained Forever*. New York: Viking Penguin, 1991.

Sequencing

Sequencing Mini-Lesson 1

Sequencing Guidelines

Opening the Lesson

- In preparation for this activity, I cut apart a comic strip for each pair of students. I write a number on the back of each panel that corresponds to its order in the strip so that my students can check their work. Then I place each cut-up comic strip in an envelope.

Idea

Before cutting apart the panels, turn over the comic strip and write a word on the back of it. One letter should appear on the back of each panel. When the panels have been placed in order, tell students to turn them over to make sure the letters form a word.

- After pairing my students, I challenge them to put their comic strip panels in sequential order.
- Then the partners present their sequenced comic strips to the rest of the class, and we discuss what kinds of strategies they used to place the panels in the correct order.

Teaching the Lesson

1. Begin by giving a definition of sequencing. Here's what I tell my class: *Sequencing is bringing order to a group of ideas, items, or processes. It involves looking closely at the steps or events and finding a logical and meaningful order in which to place them.* Give the comic-strip activity they've completed as a concrete example of sequencing. Ask students to shorten the definition and rephrase it in their own words.
2. Then write these guidelines on the chalkboard, and discuss them:
   - Read through all the steps (or events) so that you can identify the end result for the sequencing.
   - Decide which steps (or events) are first and last.
   - Arrange the remaining steps (or events) in the correct order.
   - Check to see if any steps (or events) are missing or left out.
   - Evaluate the final arrangement of steps (or events) to see if it makes sense.

Objective

Students use sequencing guidelines to arrange items in the correct order.

Materials

1 comic strip and 3 envelopes for each pair of students, scissors, markers, *The Polar Express* by Chris Van Allsburg (Houghton Mifflin, 1985)

Reproducibles

(Make 1 copy for each pair of students.)

Story Strips for *The Polar Express*, page 9

Sequencing Guidelines Sheet, page 10

"How-to" Sequence Strips, page 11

3. Give students a chance to practice using the guidelines. (NOTE: For this activity, you will need to make enough copies of the Story Strips for *The Polar Express* for each pair of students.) Cut apart the story strips, and place the sets into envelopes. Read aloud *The Polar Express*. Then pass out the Sequencing Guidelines Sheet and envelopes to partners. Tell students to place the story strips in chronological order. As they complete each step on the guidelines sheet, they should check it off. Set a timer for five minutes, and set partners to work. Go over the correct sequence of the story strips. Ask students how the guidelines helped them.

4. For the next activity, enlarge and make enough copies of the "How-to" Sequence Strips reproducible so that each pair will have a set for one of the four activities. Cut apart the strips, and place the sets in envelopes. Again, partners will put the strips in order and check off the steps on the guidelines sheet. Have a complete set of "How-to" Sequence Strips at your desk to use as answer keys. As they finish the task, partners can check their work against the answer key.

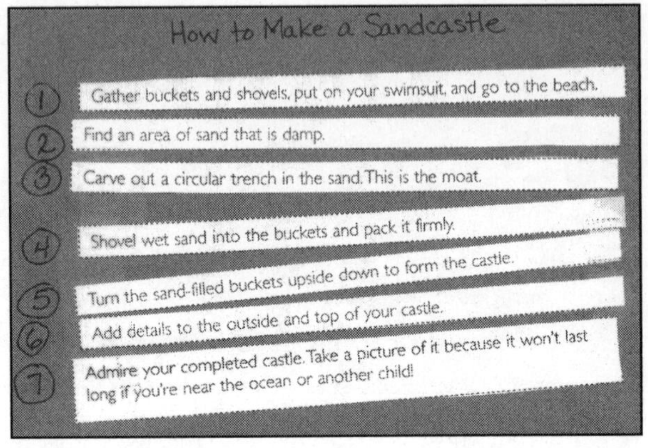

NOTE: There are two sets of checklists for the How-to activities on the guidelines sheet. The extra checklist can be used for pairs to practice sequencing a second activity from the "How-to" Sequence Strips reproducible, or students can use it when they order classmates' how-to strips in the Opening the Lesson activity on page 12.

Closing the Lesson

Use one or more of these activities to wrap up the mini-lesson.

- **Journal:** Have students write their own definitions of sequencing. Ask how they use sequencing in their everyday lives and why it is an important strategy to know.
- **Assessment:** Instruct students to write out their own "How-to" sequence strips for a familiar activitiy. Encourage them to include as many as eight steps. They should cut apart the strips and place them in an envelope labeled with "How-to Activity" and their names. Remind students to make an answer key. They will use these strips in Mini-Lesson 2.

Name ______________________ Date ______________

Story Strips for *The Polar Express*

To the teacher: Make a copy for each pair of students. Cut up the story strips and place them in an envelope. Give an envelope to each pair. This sheet is the answer key; the strips are written in chronological order.

The boy heard the sounds of hissing steam and squeaking metal late on Christmas Eve.

A train was going to the North Pole, and the conductor invited the boy aboard, even though the boy was in his pajamas.

The children on the train sang Christmas carols, ate candy, and drank hot cocoa.

The Polar Express took the children though cold, dark forests where wolves roamed.

The train even climbed high along mountaintops and then took the children across a barren desert of ice.

The conductor pointed to the North Pole, which was a huge city filled with factories, at the top of the world.

The conductor told the children that one of them would receive the first gift of Christmas.

After the children saw thousands of elves, the train stopped and unloaded everyone.

Santa asked the boy what he wanted for Christmas, and the boy said a bell from Santa's sleigh.

The boy received the first gift of Christmas, but the bell fell out of a hole in his pants.

Santa found the bell, placed it in a small box, and set it under the boy's Christmas tree. He left a note telling the boy to fix his pants.

After many years, only the boy could hear the bell ring.

Name ______________________________ Date ______________

Sequencing Guidelines Sheet

Use these guidelines to help you sequence. Check off each step as you complete it.

The Polar Express

_____ **1.** Read through all the steps (or events) so that you can identify the end result for the sequencing.

_____ **2.** Decide which steps are first and last.

_____ **3.** Arrange the remaining steps in the correct order.

_____ **4.** Check to see if any steps are missing or left out.

_____ **5.** Evaluate the final arrangement of steps to see if it makes sense.

_____ **6.** Did you place the strips in the correct order? (Check with the answer key.)

How-to Activity: ______________________________

_____ **1.** Read through all the steps (or events) so that you can identify the end result for the sequencing.

_____ **2.** Decide which steps are first and last.

_____ **3.** Arrange the remaining steps in the correct order.

_____ **4.** Check to see if any steps are missing or left out.

_____ **5.** Evaluate the final arrangement of steps to see if it makes sense.

_____ **6.** Did you place the strips in the correct order? (Check with the answer key.)

How-to Activity: ______________________________

_____ **1.** Read through all the steps (or events) so that you can identify the end result for the sequencing.

_____ **2.** Decide which steps are first and last.

_____ **3.** Arrange the remaining steps in the correct order.

_____ **4.** Check to see if any steps are missing or left out.

_____ **5.** Evaluate the final arrangement of steps to see if it makes sense.

_____ **6.** Did you place the strips in the correct order? (Check with the answer key.)

Name ______________________ Date ______________

"How-to" Sequence Strips

To the teacher: Enlarge this page to 150% to make it easy to cut apart the strips. Cut along the dotted lines, and place each set of strips in a separate envelope. This sheet is the answer key; the strips are written in chronological order.

Activity 1: How to Wash a Vehicle	Activity 3: How to Ride a Bicycle
Set out the supplies you're going to use.	Remove the training wheels from your bicycle.
Vacuum the inside of the car to remove dirt.	Put on your helmet.
Spray the outside of the vehicle with a hose.	Make sure you know where the brakes are and how to use them.
Dip a sponge into soapy water and scrub the vehicle.	Straddle the bike and hold on to the handle bars.
Rinse the soapy water off the vehicle with a hose.	Have someone hold the bicycle from behind while you sit on the seat.
Wipe the windows dry with a special, no-streak towel.	Start pedaling and steering the bike.
Do spot cleaning on any areas you missed.	Ring your bell if anything gets in your way.
Admire your beautifully clean vehicle.	Feel proud because you just took the first steps in riding a bike by yourself.

Activity 2: How to Grow a Garden	Activity 4: How to Build a Sand Castle
Till the ground until the soil is loose.	Gather buckets and shovels, put on your swimsuit, and go to the beach.
Add more soil if you need it, and fertilizer.	Find an area of sand that is damp.
Smooth and level the ground with a rake.	Carve out a circular trench in the sand. This is the moat.
Use a string line to make straight rows.	Shovel wet sand into the buckets and pack it firmly.
Dig a small trench, plant seeds, and cover them with soil.	Turn the sand-filled buckets upside down to form the castle.
Carefully water the new plants.	Add details to the outside and top of your castle.
Hoe or pull weeds around plants.	Admire your completed castle. Take a picture of it, because it won't last long if you're near the ocean or another child!
Enjoy your flowers or vegetables!	

Sequencing Visuals

Objective

Students select and work with a visual organizer to sequence information from a book.

Materials

a variety of short stories, folk tales, and non-fiction articles; passages from social studies textbooks that contain dates; paper and pens

Reproducibles

Sequencing Guidelines Sheet, page 10

Sequencing Visuals: (Make 1 transparency of each. Make copies as requested by your students.)

Box-to-Box Sequencing Visual, page 14

Ladder Sequencing Visual, page 15

Stair Step Sequencing Visual, page 16

"S" Sequencing Visual, page 17

Vertical Time Line Sequencing Visual, page 18

Horizontal Time Line Sequencing Visual, page 19

Opening the Lesson

- To open this lesson, I review with my students the five sequencing guideline steps that were introduced in Mini-Lesson 1.
- Then I ask students to exchange their "How-to Activity" envelopes (see Assessment activity, page 8) and put the activities in the correct sequence. As they work, they complete the last section of the Sequencing Guidelines Sheet. Then I ask partners to use their answer keys to check each other's work. I encourage them to give each other feedback about which clues were helpful and which were confusing.

Teaching the Lesson

1. Introduce each sequencing visual reproducible (pages 14–19), and discuss it. Point out to students that one sequencing visual may work better than another, depending upon the type of information they are sequencing. For instance, when sequencing dates and events, they should use either of the time-line visuals.

Here's how I present the horizontal time-line visual to my students: *I used the horizontal time line to sequence the events presented in chapter 14 of our social studies book. If you remember, that chapter was about the American frontier. I went through the chapter and wrote down the most important events and their dates. Then I wrote them in order on the visual. The first entry is 1859, when the Comstock lode was discovered. The next event occurred in 1862, when the Homestead Act was passed. In 1869, the first transcontinental railroad was completed. Seven years later, in 1876, the Battle of Little Big Horn was fought. The Dawes Act was passed in 1887. Finally, in 1890, the Director of the U.S. Census declared that the American frontier was closed. If I wanted to write more information about each event, I would use the vertical time-line visual because it offers a little more space.*

While all of the reproducible pages are suitable for use with any sequencing activity, each offers a slightly different organizing focus that you can use to support specific types of assignments. Here are some ideas for using the other visuals:

Box-to-Box presents a descending column of boxes that is ideal for plotting a story line or listing a series of past events that lead to a current event.

Ladder provides a frame for a sequence of cumulative events that build toward a single, final event.

Stair Step introduces the concept of growth or decline, as in the events that propelled the Civil Rights movement forward. Using arrows or numbers in the steps shows whether the event sequence is moving forward or backward in time.

"S" shows how events might alternate between positive and negative or suggests cause-and-effect relationships between events.

2. Have students choose one of the sequencing visuals to graph the events in a short story, a folk tale, or a non-fiction article. Suggest that first they write down the main events from their reading and then write the events in order on the visual. You may make copies of the visuals or have students draw them.

> **Tip**
>
> To help my students visualize how to use each sequencing visual most effectively, I create examples for them by sequencing events from books we've recently read on the sequencing visual transparencies. The material is still fresh in their minds, and they can see how the major events fit in the visuals.

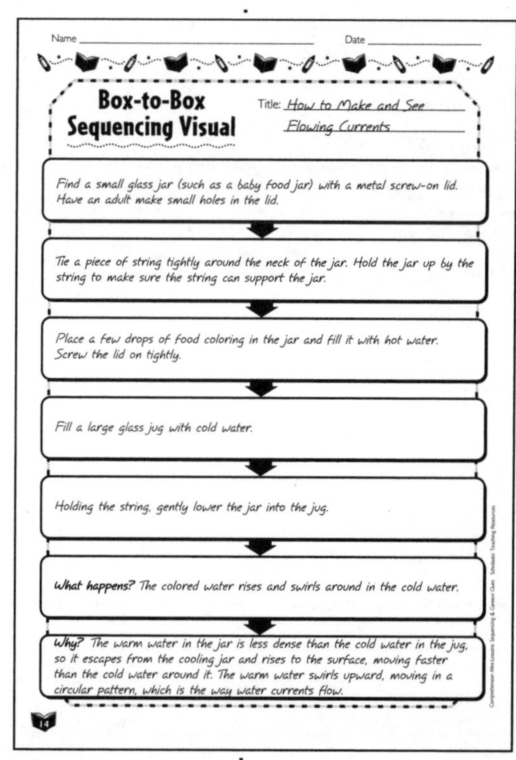

Name ______________ Date ______________

Box-to-Box Sequencing Visual

Title: *How to Make and See Flowing Currents*

Find a small glass jar (such as a baby food jar) with a metal screw-on lid. Have an adult make small holes in the lid.

Tie a piece of string tightly around the neck of the jar. Hold the jar up by the string to make sure the string can support the jar.

Place a few drops of food coloring in the jar and fill it with hot water. Screw the lid on tightly.

Fill a large glass jug with cold water.

Holding the string, gently lower the jar into the jug.

***What happens?** The colored water rises and swirls around in the cold water.*

***Why?** The warm water in the jar is less dense than the cold water in the jug, so it escapes from the cooling jar and rises to the surface, moving faster than the cold water around it. The warm water swirls upward, moving in a circular pattern, which is the way water currents flow.*

14

Closing the Lesson

Use one or more of these activities to wrap up the mini-lesson.

- **Assessment:** Have students select and then graph passages from their social studies text-books on sequencing visuals. Let pairs exchange visuals and check each other's work.
- **Journal:** Challenge students to show how they could use a sequencing visual to write an outline of a short story they wanted to write. To extend the activity, ask them to use the visual to write their stories.

Name ______________________________ Date ______________

Box-to-Box Sequencing Visual

Title: ______________________________

____

Comprehension Mini-Lessons: Sequencing & Context Clues Scholastic Teaching Resources

Name ______________________ Date ______________

Ladder Sequencing Visual

Title: ______________________

____

Name ____________________ Date ____________________

Title: ____________________

____

Stair Step Sequencing Visual

Name ____________________ Date ____________________

"S" Sequencing Visual

Title: ____________________

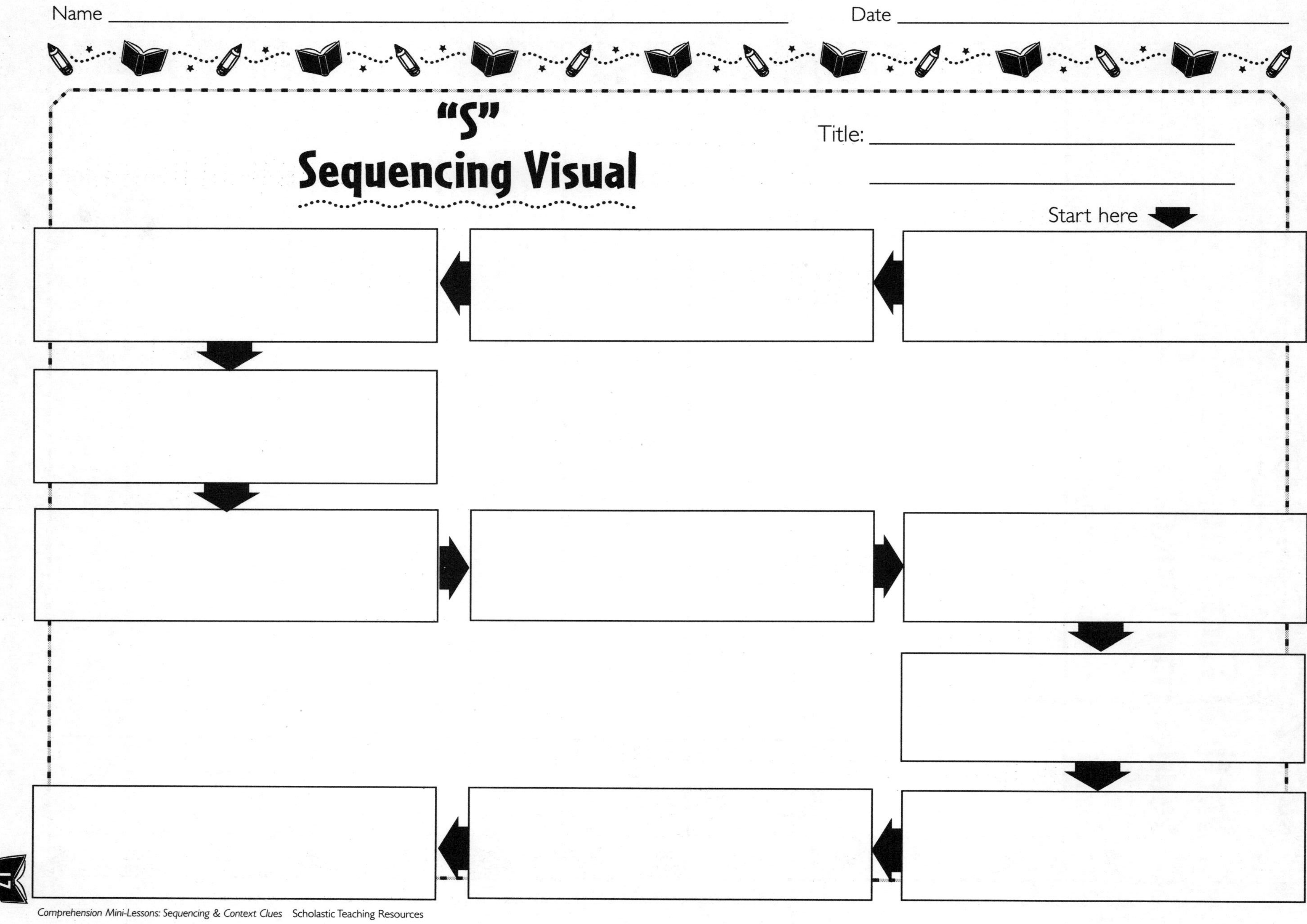

Name ______________________________ Date ______________

Vertical Time Line Sequencing Visual

Title: ______________________________

____

DATE	EVENT DESCRIPTION

Name ______________________ Date ______________

Horizontal Time Line Sequencing Visual

Title: ______________________

____

DATE

EVENT

How-to Expository Writing

Objective

Students learn transition words and apply guidelines to write how-to expository essays.

Materials

"how-to" books such as *How to Dig a Hole to the Other Side of the World* by Faith McNulty (Scott Foresman, 1990) or *How to Eat Fried Worms* by Thomas Rockwell (Yearling Books, 1953)

Reproducibles

List of Transition Words, page 22 (Make 1 copy for each student.)

Brainstorming Sheet for How-to Writing, page 23 (Make 1 copy for each student.)

How-to Writing Rubric, page 24 (Make 1 copy for each student.)

Opening the Lesson

- To give my students a taste of sequence in expository writing, I read aloud one or more humorous "how-to" books such as *How to Eat Fried Worms* or *How to Dig a Hole to the Other Side of the World.*
- Then we discuss what makes these books good examples of sequence: 1) the writers use key words such as *next, finally, first;* 2) they include a series of steps or directions to follow; and 3) a goal is reached only by successfully following the steps or directions in chronological order.

Teaching the Lesson

1. Now students will have the opportunity to try their hands at how-to expository writing. Begin the activity by introducing the following information about this type of expository writing:

- *The introduction should introduce the topic and immediately grab the reader's attention. These "grabbers" may include a quotation, a startling comment, or a brief narrative.*
- *The body of the writing should include the steps in the how-to process. Elaborate each step so that the reader can visualize it. It's also vital that the steps be accurate. Writers must be sure to carefully research their topics before they begin writing.*
- *The steps should be in sequential order. The reader should not have to "double back."*
- *All of the steps should be included and described fully. The reader should not have to make inferences about what he or she should do next.*
- *Key words that signal a new step are important. These key words are called transition words. They tell the reader the order in which steps should occur or how one idea is related to another.*

- *The conclusion refers back to the introduction and presents the goal.*

2. Distribute the reproducibles to students before they begin writing. They should keep the List of Transition Words reproducible in their writing portfolios so they can easily refer to it. The Brainstorming Sheet helps students begin the writing process by reminding them to think about how they will grab their audience's attention, how they will order the steps or directions, which transition words they plan to use, and how they will conclude their writing. The Evaluation Rubric reminds students what is required of them while they are writing. Encourage students to keep these reproducibles on their desks and to refer to them frequently to stay on track.

Idea

Write and share with the class your own humorous how-to essay for an activity you enjoy and to which students will also relate (e.g., how to tell a good joke or how to get ready for school in the morning). After reading it aloud, go through the work and point out how it conforms to the guidelines.

Closing the Lesson

Use one or more of these activities to wrap up the mini-lesson.

- **Verbal/Auditory:** Allow class time for students to read aloud their work. This is a good time for you to use the rubrics to assess their writing.
- **Spatial/Visual:** Have students write a how-to expository piece on giving directions. They should select a starting point and ending point. Remind them to write the correct names of the streets and use the appropriate spatial and positioning words such as *right*, *left*, *north*, *south*, *east*, and *west*. Encourage them to draw maps to accompany their text. This will also provide a way of checking their text.

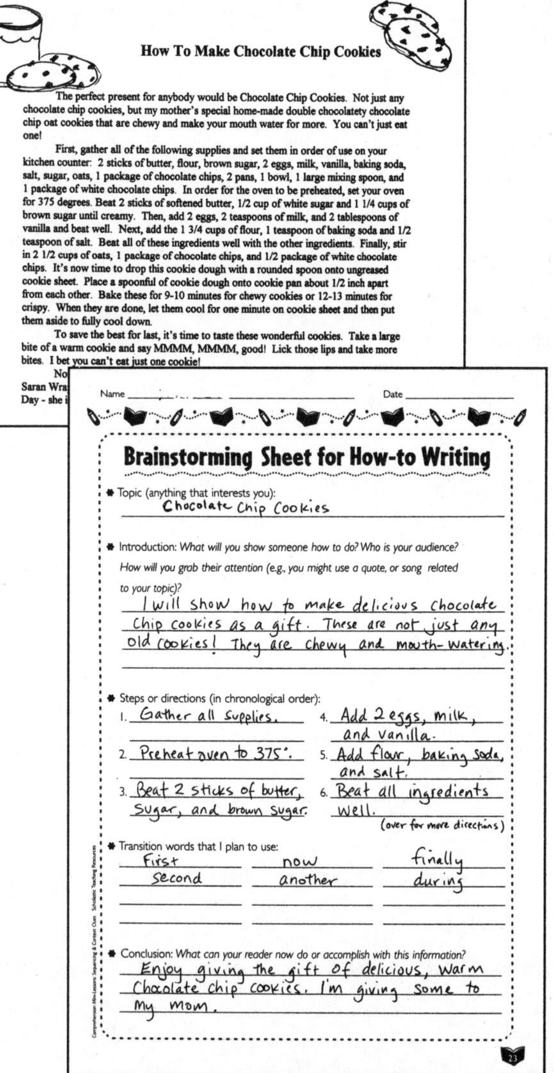

How To Make Chocolate Chip Cookies

The perfect present for anybody would be Chocolate Chip Cookies. Not just any chocolate chip cookies, but my mother's special home-made double chocolatety chocolate chip oat cookies that are chewy and make your mouth water for more. You can't just eat one!

First, gather all of the following supplies and set them in order of use on your kitchen counter: 2 sticks of butter, flour, brown sugar, 2 eggs, milk, vanilla, baking soda, salt, sugar, oats, 1 package of chocolate chips, 2 pans, 1 bowl, 1 large mixing spoon, and 1 package of white chocolate chips. In order for the oven to be preheated, set your oven for 375 degrees. Beat 2 sticks of softened butter, 1/2 cup of white sugar and 1 1/4 cups of brown sugar until creamy. Then, add 2 eggs, 2 teaspoons of milk, and 2 tablespoons of vanilla and beat well. Next, add the 1 3/4 cups of flour, 1 teaspoon of baking soda and 1/2 teaspoon of salt. Beat all of these ingredients well with the other ingredients. Finally, stir in 2 1/2 cups of oats, 1 package of chocolate chips, and 1/2 package of white chocolate chips. It's now time to drop this cookie dough with a rounded spoon onto ungreased cookie sheet. Place a spoonful of cookie dough onto cookie pan about 1/2 inch apart from each other. Bake these for 9-10 minutes for chewy cookies or 12-13 minutes for crispy. When they are done, let them cool for one minute on cookie sheet and then put them aside to fully cool down.

To save the best for last, it's time to taste these wonderful cookies. Take a large bite of a warm cookie and say MMMM, MMMM, good! Lick those lips and take more bites. I bet you can't eat just one cookie!

No

Saran Wra

Day - she i

Name ______ Date ______

Brainstorming Sheet for How-to Writing

- Topic (anything that interests you): Chocolate Chip Cookies
- Introduction: *What will you show someone how to do? Who is your audience? How will you grab their attention (e.g., you might use a quote, or song related to your topic)?* I will show how to make delicious chocolate chip cookies as a gift. These are not just any old cookies! They are chewy and mouth-watering.
- Steps or directions (in chronological order):
  1. Gather all supplies.
  2. Preheat oven to 375°.
  3. Beat 2 sticks of butter, sugar, and brown sugar.
  4. Add 2 eggs, milk, and vanilla.
  5. Add flour, baking soda, and salt.
  6. Beat all ingredients well.

  (over for more directions)
- Transition words that I plan to use: First, second, now, another, finally, during
- Conclusion: *What can your reader now do or accomplish with this information?* Enjoy giving the gift of delicious, warm chocolate chip cookies. I'm giving some to my mom.

Comprehension Mini-Lessons: Sequencing & Context Clues Scholastic Teaching Resources

23

Name ______________________ Date ______________

List of Transition Words

Words That Show Time

about	during	until	yesterday
finally	after	first	meanwhile
next	then	at	second
today	soon	as soon as	before
third	tomorrow	later	when
earlier	slowly	eventually	suddenly
quickly	all at once		

Words That Move to the Next Idea

also	finally	in addition	in conclusion
another	then	to sum up	furthermore
to begin with	first, second, etc.	moreover	besides

Words That Show Results or Conclusions

as a result	finally	consequently	in conclusion
therefore	last	in summary	to summarize

Words That Show Contrast (Differences)

however	in spite of	instead	nevertheless
on the other hand	although	but	yet
otherwise	even though		

Words That Show Comparison (Similarities)

likewise	as	similarly	like
in the same way	also		

Name ______________________ Date ______________

Brainstorming Sheet for How-to Writing

✱ Topic (anything that interests you):

____

✱ Introduction: *What will you show someone how to do? Who is your audience? How will you grab their attention (e.g., you might use a quote or song related to your topic)?*

____

____

____

____

✱ Steps or directions (in chronological order):

1. ______________________ 4. ______________________

2. ______________________ 5. ______________________

3. ______________________ 6. ______________________

✱ Transition words that I plan to use:

___________ ___________ ___________

___________ ___________ ___________

___________ ___________ ___________

___________ ___________ ___________

✱ Conclusion: *What can your reader now do or accomplish with this information?*

____

____

____

____

How-to Writing Rubric

Student's Name ______________________________

CRITERIA	Incomplete 0	Okay 1	Good 2	Outstanding 3
Style and Structure **1.** The introduction states the purpose of the writing and grabs the reader's attention. **2.** The conclusion refers back to the introduction and states the goal of the how-to topic. **3.** Each step is in the correct sequential order. **4.** Each step is fully elaborated so that it's clear to the reader. **5.** None of the steps is missing. **6.** Transition words are used often and appropriately. **7.** Detail words and new vocabulary are used throughout the writing. **Presentation** **8.** The essay is edited. (Spelling, punctuation, capitalization, and grammar have been checked and corrected.)				
Things you did well:				
Opportunities for growth:				
TOTAL SCORE:				_______ /24

Sequencing Mini-Lesson 4

Create-a-Play

Opening the Lesson

- Writing dialogue and acting out steps for an activity can really bring an activity to life for students. Moreover, communicating how to do something through dialogue and gesture can underscore for students the importance of communicating clearly to an audience how to sequence steps in a process and describe those steps adequately. To prepare my students for writing their own how-to plays, I ask for eight volunteers to put on a production of the play, "How to Make Coins." After assigning parts, I allow the cast time to read through and rehearse the play once. I also supply the magnifying glasses and any other reasonable props my students suggest.
- Then I set aside class time for the actual performance. Afterward, I ask the audience to write reviews of the play, including what they learned, what they liked about the play, and what they would improve. I collect their reviews in a binder and keep it available so that everyone can have the chance to study the comments. It's also helpful to place a copy of the play in the binder, too. Writing a review helps students think critically about how the how-to activity was presented—chronology, transition, detail of execution—all of which they can apply to their expository writing.

Teaching the Lesson

1. Select five play topics for groups of 3–5 students to write about. Choose educational topics that are interesting to your class and fit your curriculum. For my fifth-grade class I suggested How Paper Is Made, How Coca-Cola Is Made, How Rocks Are Formed, How a Muscle Works, and How Water Is Cleaned and Recycled. Provide resource material so that students can direct their energy to writing and performing their plays.
2. Write the following guidelines for the plays on the chalkboard:
   - Each student in the group must contribute at least two lines

Objective

Groups write plays that show how to do something in sequential order.

Materials

magnifying glass, resources such as *How Come?* by Kathy Wollard (Workman, 1993), miscellaneous props, costumes, and other materials

Reproducibles

How to Make Coins play, pp. 27–28 (Make 9 copies—8 for the cast, 1 for you.)

to the play. Write your initials next to your lines. You may have one group member write out the play.

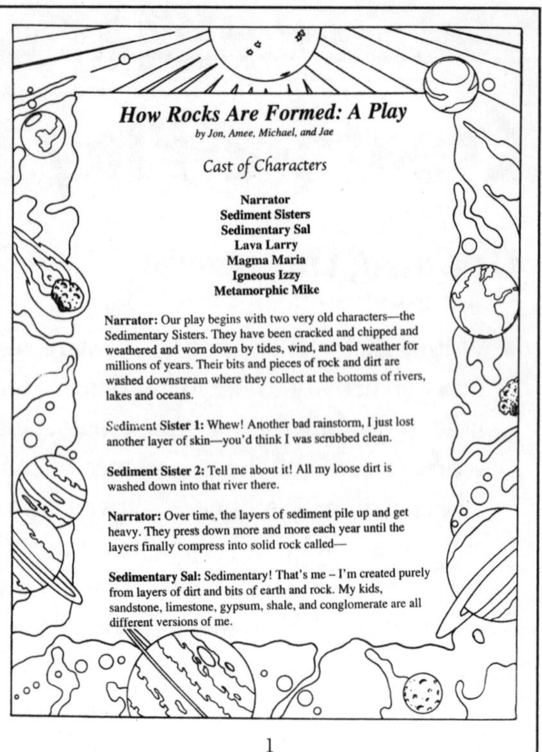

How Rocks Are Formed: A Play

by Jon, Amee, Michael, and Jae

Cast of Characters

Narrator
Sediment Sisters
Sedimentary Sal
Lava Larry
Magma Maria
Igneous Izzy
Metamorphic Mike

Narrator: Our play begins with two very old characters—the Sedimentary Sisters. They have been cracked and chipped and weathered and worn down by tides, wind, and bad weather for millions of years. Their bits and pieces of rock and dirt are washed downstream where they collect at the bottoms of rivers, lakes and oceans.

Sediment Sister 1: Whew! Another bad rainstorm, I just lost another layer of skin—you'd think I was scrubbed clean.

Sediment Sister 2: Tell me about it! All my loose dirt is washed down into that river there.

Narrator: Over time, the layers of sediment pile up and get heavy. They press down more and more each year until the layers finally compress into solid rock called—

Sedimentary Sal: Sedimentary! That's me – I'm created purely from layers of dirt and bits of earth and rock. My kids, sandstone, limestone, gypsum, shale, and conglomerate are all different versions of me.

1

- Each student must have a role in the play. This means that some of you may have more than one role.
- Be creative! Be humorous! You can bring inanimate objects to life!
- You must FULLY describe the process in your play.
- You must SHOW and SAY how the process works—in sequential order.
- The play should be two to three pages long. If possible, type your play. I'll make duplicates so that each student in the group has a copy of the play. (Try to memorize your lines!)
- Make a list of your props and costumes. I'll help you obtain these things.

Closing the Lesson

Use one or more of these activities to wrap up the mini-lesson.

- **Verbal/Auditory:** Hold performances of the plays in your classroom. Consider putting the shows on the road—let your playwrights/actors perform for other classes.
- **Journal:** Ask students to reflect on their experiences as writers and performers. Could they write a how-to expository piece on how to write or put on a play?

Name ______________________ Date ______________

How to Make Coins: A Play

Cast of Characters (in order of appearance):

Narrator	Riddler	Inspector
Blanking Press	Upsetter	Count&Bag
Heatwashdry	Minter	

Narrator: I wanted to share with you the best field trip I have ever taken. Mrs. Riney took us, the coolest fifth-grade class, to the Money Machine in Denver, Colorado. We also did some snow skiing in our spare time. Anyway, you won't believe it, but this Money Machine came alive and told us how it worked. The funniest part of the machine was the Riddler. He kept laughing the whole time. You'll see. I videotaped it all for you to see. Ready? Here goes—here is how the spare change in your pocket is made.

Narrator pantomimes using a video camera. He "films" the characters throughout the play.

Blanking Press: *(acts very strong and tough)* Hi! I'm the Blanking Press. I'm so strong—see my muscles? *(flexes muscles)* I take in long sheets of metal and punch out round discs called blanks. You see, I start the whole coining process. I love punching things out. I send these blanks to be heated, washed, and dried.

Heatwashdry: *(acts very motherly)* I'll take it over from here, Blanking Press. Just leave it to me to take care of all the little ones. I heat the blanks until they're soft. Then, in order to make sure they're squeaky clean, I wash and dry them. I have to make sure they don't get dirty again. Next, I send the shiny blanks to the Riddler. He will crack you up.

Riddler: *(acts very energetic)* It's about time! You'd think that they were the most important machines around. But, *I* am! My name is Mr. Riddler, but you can call me Riddler.
(He dances up and down and sings this song.)
I feel good—nah-nah-nah-nah-nah-nah-nah
Like I knew that I would now— nah-nah-nah-nah-nah-nah-nah
I feel good— nah-nah-nah-nah-nah-nah-nah
From my head to my shoes now— nah-nah-nah-nah-nah-nah-nah
So good, so good, I've got it good—da-da-da-da-da

Comprehension Mini-Lessons: Sequencing & Context Clues Scholastic Teaching Resources

Name ______________________ Date ______________

How to Make Coins: A Play (Cont.)

Riddler: You see, I do a lot of shakin'! I sort the blanks to screen out any disks that are the wrong size or shape. I pick out the best ones. The rejects fall away. They're chopped up and reused.

Upsetter: Hey, Riddler, you're starting to upset me—you don't want to do that.

Riddler: Oh, you're always upset, so who cares? You're just jealous because I have such an important role.

Upsetter: *(acts like a goody two-shoes)* I'm really not upset all the time, but my name is Upsetter. I set all the coins UP. I think this is a very important role. I raise a rim around the edges of the blanks. Go ahead and look at a coin. I make the edges smooth! I do such a good job! Don't you think I do?

Minter: *(stamps feet)* Some people call me the bug killer, but my real name is the Minter. No, I don't smell like mint, although I wouldn't mind. After the Upsetter puts edges on the blanks, I receive the blanks and stamp coin designs on each side of them at the same time. Aren't I talented? I am the most artistic one around here. I get to create the artwork on stamps, too. I can tell you every logo on every coin.

Inspector: *(holds up magnifying glass)* Oh, Minter, stop bragging. You make some mistakes now and then. In fact, it's my job to find those mistakes. Some coins are totally discarded because the Minter messed up so badly. The decent ones move on to the next step.

Count&Bag: One, two, three, four, five, six, seven, eight, nine, ten—oh, hello! As you can tell, it's my job to count the coins and then drop them into large canvas bags. I seal the bags shut and send them to the Federal Reserve Banks. If I count wrong, I could lose my job, so I am very careful—especially with the quarters.

Narrator: Well, I hope you enjoyed the video. As you can tell, they all have to work well together to accomplish the job of creating our coin currency.

Sequencing Mini-Lesson 

Test-Taking Format

Objective

Students apply sequencing rules to answer sample multiple-choice test items.

Materials

blank transparency (optional)

Reproducibles

Sequencing Rules, page 31 (Make 1 copy for each student. Make 1 transparency.)

Sequencing Practice Paragraphs, page 32 (Make 1 copy for each student.)

Sequencing Practice Passage, page 33 (Make 1 copy for each student.)

Opening the Lesson

- To review sequencing, I write the following sentences on the board or on a transparency and display it (correct order is indicated in parentheses):

  ___ Dig a two-inch hole in the loose ground for each tomato plant. (3)

  ___ Gather all the materials you'll need to plant the tomatoes. (1)

  ___ Water the plants daily and pick any weeds that grow around them. (7)

  ___ Use your fingers to press the soil firmly around the base of each plant. (6)

  ___ Place a tomato plant into each hole. (4)

  ___ Hoe topsoil and fertilizer into the soil until the ground is loose enough to plant the tomato plants. (2)

  ___ Fill the hole around the plant with topsoil. (5)

  ___ Pick the delicious tomatoes when they are red. (8)

- Then I tell my students that the sentences tell how to plant tomatoes, but the steps are out of order. After giving them a few moments to read the steps, I ask for help in putting the steps in the correct order. As my students order the steps, I place the numbers 1–8 in each blank to indicate the sequence.
- Finally I call on volunteers to read aloud the steps using transition words; for instance, "First, gather all the materials you'll need to plant the tomatoes."

Teaching the Lesson

1. Remind students about the power of transition words, and review the words. As they read, these words will help them determine the order in which events happened. Knowing this will enable them to understand other elements in the text.
2. Display the Sequencing Rules transparency on the overhead.

Also distribute copies of the page to your students. Begin by reading aloud each rule. Then go over the example to show how the rules were put into practice. Ask students to follow your steps as you think aloud: *The question asks what Mary did after she dropped her treat. I know that the word* after *is the important word in the question, so I'll circle it. Then I'll underline the phrase* she dropped her treat *because I want to find out what happened after that event. I see the phrase in the passage, so I'll underline that, too. Since I'm looking for events after that, I'll draw an arrow down from that point. Now I'll compare the answer choices to the text next to the arrow. Only answer choice C happened after Mary dropped her treat.*

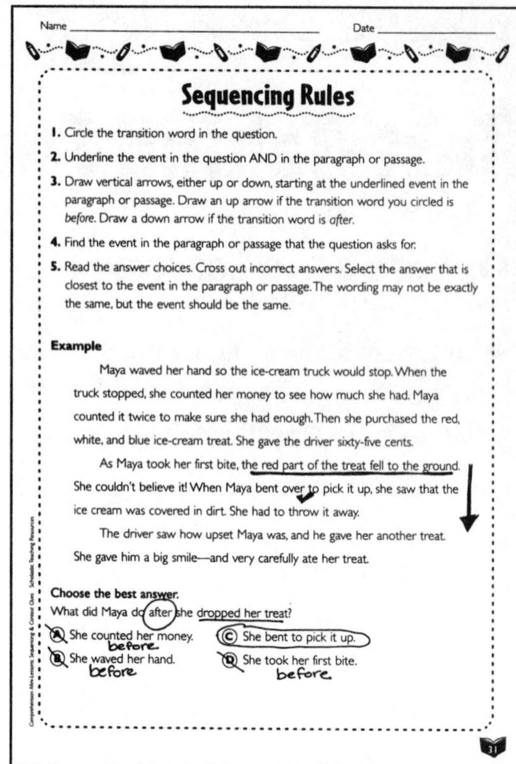

Name ____________ Date ____________

Sequencing Rules

1. Circle the transition word in the question.

2. Underline the event in the question AND in the paragraph or passage.

3. Draw vertical arrows, either up or down, starting at the underlined event in the paragraph or passage. Draw an up arrow if the transition word you circled is *before*. Draw a down arrow if the transition word is *after*.

4. Find the event in the paragraph or passage that the question asks for.

5. Read the answer choices. Cross out incorrect answers. Select the answer that is closest to the event in the paragraph or passage. The wording may not be exactly the same, but the event should be the same.

Example

Maya waved her hand so the ice-cream truck would stop. When the truck stopped, she counted her money to see how much she had. Maya counted it twice to make sure she had enough. Then she purchased the red, white, and blue ice-cream treat. She gave the driver sixty-five cents.

As Maya took her first bite, the red part of the treat fell to the ground. She couldn't believe it! When Maya bent over to pick it up, she saw that the ice cream was covered in dirt. She had to throw it away.

The driver saw how upset Maya was, and he gave her another treat. She gave him a big smile—and very carefully ate her treat.

Choose the best answer.

What did Maya do after she dropped her treat?

Ⓐ She counted her money. before
Ⓒ She bent to pick it up.
Ⓑ She waved her hand. before
Ⓓ She took her first bite. before

31

3. You may want to highlight the key phrase *immediately after* in the first example on page 32. Students should be able to tell you that of the three answer choices showing events after Grace went upstairs (B, C, and D), only C gives the event that happened directly after the event in question. Encourage students to act like sleuths in picking out key words in the question.

4. Let pairs of students practice the sequencing rules by working together to complete the Sequencing Practice Paragraphs reproducible. It's very important that each partner understand and practice the rules. Set aside time to go over and discuss the correct answers. How did the sequencing rules help them determine the best answers?

Closing the Lesson

Use one or more of these activities to wrap up the mini-lesson.

- **Assessment:** Have students complete the Sequencing Practice Passage: Baking Bread reproducible independently.
- **Students Working Together:** Challenge students to write half- to one-page short stories and at least two sequencing questions. Let them exchange stories with partners and use the sequencing rules to answer the questions.

Answers

Sequencing Practice Paragraphs, page 32: D; B

Sequencing Practice Passage: Baking Bread, page 33: 1. D; 2. C; 3. D; 4. B

Name ______________________ Date ______________

Sequencing Rules

1. Circle the transition word in the question.

2. Underline the event in the question AND in the paragraph or passage.

3. Draw vertical arrows, either up or down, starting at the underlined event in the paragraph or passage. Draw an up arrow if the transition word you circled is *before*. Draw a down arrow if the transition word is *after*.

4. Find the event in the paragraph or passage that the question asks for.

5. Read the answer choices. Cross out incorrect answers. Select the answer that is closest to the event in the paragraph or passage. The wording may not be exactly the same, but the event should be the same.

Example

Maya waved her hand so that the ice-cream truck would stop. When the truck stopped, she counted her money to see how much she had. Maya counted it twice to make sure she had enough. Then she purchased the red, white, and blue ice-cream treat. She gave the driver sixty-five cents.

As Maya took her first bite, the red part of the treat fell to the ground. She couldn't believe it! When Maya bent over to pick it up, she saw that the ice cream was covered in dirt. She had to throw it away.

The driver saw how upset Maya was, and he gave her another treat. She gave him a big smile—and very carefully ate her treat.

Choose the best answer.

What did Maya do after she dropped her treat?

Ⓐ She counted her money.

Ⓑ She waved her hand.

Ⓒ She bent to pick it up.

Ⓓ She took her first bite.

Name ______________________ Date ______________

Sequencing Practice Paragraphs

Use the sequencing rules to answer the question. Mark the paragraph to show your work.

Grace loved playing in the sand box after school. Every day when she got home, she ran into the kitchen and grabbed a snack. Then she hurried upstairs to her bedroom to change into play clothes and sandals. After changing clothes, Grace headed for the sand box. She practically dove into the sand. Usually, Grace played with the big Tonka truck first. Next she'd shovel sand into a large bucket. Grace always played in the sand for about an hour.

Choose the best answer.

What did Grace do immediately after she went upstairs?

Ⓐ She shoveled sand into a large bucket.

Ⓑ She dove into the sand.

Ⓒ She grabbed a snack.

Ⓓ She changed her clothes.

This is the same paragraph. Use the sequencing rules to answer the question. Mark this paragraph to show your work.

Grace loved playing in the sand box after school. Every day when she got home, she ran into the kitchen and grabbed a snack. Then she hurried upstairs to her bedroom to change into play clothes and sandals. After changing clothes, Grace headed for the sand box. She practically dove into the sand. Usually, Grace played with the big Tonka truck first. Next she'd shovel sand into a large bucket. Grace always played in the sand for about an hour.

Choose the best answer.

What did Grace do before she grabbed a snack?

Ⓐ She played in the sand for an hour.

Ⓑ She ran into the kitchen.

Ⓒ She headed for the sand box.

Ⓓ She hurried upstairs.

Name ______________________ Date ______________

Sequencing Practice Passage: Baking Bread

Read the passage. Then choose the best answers.

Almost everyone likes to eat bread, but not everyone knows how easy it is to make. All you need is yeast, flour, and water.

First, mix a package of yeast with two cups of warm water. Let the mixture stand until bubbles form on the surface. Then add four cups of flour, one-half cup at a time. When the dough gets too thick to stir, scrape it onto a floured board and knead it. To knead the bread, turn the dough in a circle and fold and punch it as you turn. Knead for ten minutes as you add one more cup of flour. The dough is ready when it is no longer sticky. It should feel soft and smooth.

Put the dough in a buttered bowl and cover it with a damp dish towel. Let the dough rise for an hour or more until it doubles in size. Then knead it for another minute or so and shape it into a loaf. Let the dough rise again for forty-five minutes. Pop it into a 375-degree oven and bake for forty-five minutes.

After the bread has cooled for ten minutes, slice it.

1. After the dough has doubled in size,—

Ⓐ knead it for ten minutes
Ⓑ mix the yeast with two cups of water
Ⓒ add the flour, one-half cup at a time
Ⓓ knead it and shape it into a loaf

2. Just before you knead the dough for ten minutes—

Ⓐ put it in a buttered bowl and cover with a dish towel
Ⓑ mix a package of yeast with two cups of warm water
Ⓒ scrape it onto a floured board
Ⓓ bake it for forty-five minutes at 375 degrees

3. After forming the dough into a loaf,—

Ⓐ add more flour and water
Ⓑ knead it one more time
Ⓒ cool it for ten minutes
Ⓓ let it rise again for forty-five minutes

4. What is the last step in the bread baking process described above?

Ⓐ eating it
Ⓑ slicing it
Ⓒ letting it cool
Ⓓ taking it out of the oven

Putting It All Together: Filmstrip Project

Objective

Students use sequencing skills to write and illustrate a filmstrip that explains how to do something.

Duration

one week

Materials

shoebox, 2 pencils (unsharpened) or 2 cardboard tubes from coat hangers for each student, tape or glue, markers, poster board, blank transparencies

Reproducibles

Student Project Sheet, page 35 (Make 1 copy for each student.)

Filmstrip paper, page 36 (Make 4 or more copies for each student.)

Preparing for the Project

- Use the instructions on the Student Project Sheet to make a sample filmstrip for students to examine as they work on their projects. You may also choose to assemble the projector while your class watches.
- Hang a calendar in your classroom that shows the project due dates.
- Make several film frames out of transparencies. Select a topic that's related to your curriculum, such as how a tepee is built. Draw a picture and caption on each transparency to show the process chronologically.
- Use the overhead as your film projector. Present your frames in order.

Introducing the Project

1. Explain to students that they'll be making their own filmstrips. They can choose any how-to topic that interests them as long as it has several chronological steps. Here are some ideas I've introduced in my classroom: how to make glue, how a washing machine works, how the water cycle works, how hurricanes are born, how to bake a cake, how batteries work, how coal is formed, and so on.
2. Encourage students to discuss topics with their families. Emphasize again that the topic should be interesting to them.
3. After you approve their topics, help students find library, Internet, and other types of resources for their research.
4. Distribute and discuss the Student Project Sheet. Make sure everyone understands the instructions.

Assessing the Project

- **Verbal/Auditory/Kinesthetic:** Have students present their final projects to the class. Allow time for a short discussion after each presentation. This will give you the opportunity to assess their work.

Name ______________________________ Date ______________

Filmstrip Project

Student Project Sheet

1. Choose a how-to topic that interests you. It should have several steps in sequence.

2. When you research your topic, write down 7–10 steps that are related to it. The steps should fully explain the process and they should be in the correct order. Don't leave out any steps.

3. Ask your teacher for enough copies of Filmstrip Paper to record each step in a frame of the filmstrip. Write and illustrate the steps in order on the filmstrip.

4. The text should be written clearly and neatly. Elaborate as much as possible to fully describe each step.

5. The illustrations should be colorful and neat, and help explain the text accurately.

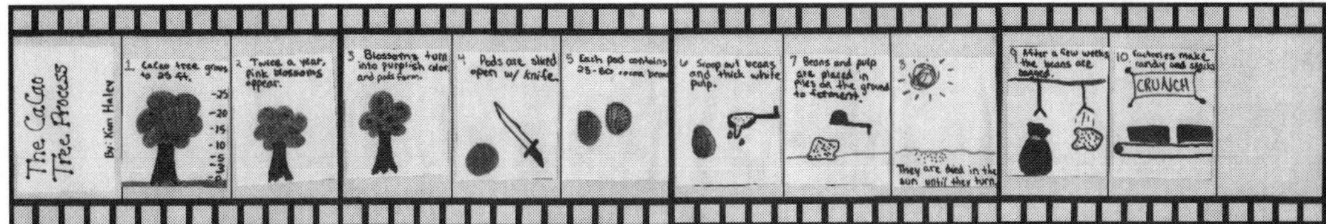

6. Attach the Filmstrip Paper pages to each other with tape or glue in order to create a continuous filmstrip.

7. Leave about 1 inch of blank space at the top and bottom of the filmstrip. Tape the top to a pencil or cardboard tube from a coat hanger. Do the same for the bottom. Make sure that your filmstrip moves as you turn the pencils or cardboard tubes.

8. Cut out a 3- by 5-inch square from the back of a shoebox so that only one filmstrip frame is displayed at a time.

9. Punch 2 pairs of holes in the sides of the shoebox—1 on each side above and 1 on each side below the cutout window. Slide the pencils or cardboard tubes into these holes.

10. Turn the pencils or cardboard tubes to show your filmstrip!

Name ______________________ Date ______________________

Context Clues

Context Clues Mini-Lesson 1

Why Use Context Clues?

Objective

Students define context clues, figure out the meaning of words using context clues, and solve word riddles.

Materials

dictionary

Reproducibles

Context Clues #1, page 40 (Make 1 transparency.)

Steps for Identifying Unfamiliar Words, page 41 (Make 1 transparency and 1 copy for each student.)

Context Clues #2, page 42 (Make 1 transparency and 1 copy for each student.)

Opening the Lesson

- I begin this mini-lesson by displaying the Context Clues #1 transparency. After reading each section aloud, I ask my students to guess the meaning of the word in italics.
- As we discuss their responses, I like to pose the following questions: *How did you come to your conclusions about the definition? Which clues led you to the word's meaning? How important were these clues?*
- At the end of the discussion, I ask my students if they think they should stop to look up every word they don't know. They usually reason that looking up every unfamiliar word can be time-consuming and unnecessary. I point out that even if they had stopped to look up the unknown words on the transparency they wouldn't have found them in a dictionary—I made them up! The clues in the sentences helped them figure out the meanings of the words.

Teaching the Lesson

1. Reiterate to students that they can figure out the meaning of an unfamiliar word by looking at its context—the words and sentences around it—for synonyms, antonyms, definitions, or by getting the general sense of the passage.
2. Then display the Steps for Identifying Unfamiliar Words transparency and distribute copies to your students. After reading aloud and discussing the steps, guide students in using them with Context Clues #2.

   Here is how I usually think aloud about the word *mariner* in the first sentence: *I'll begin by drawing a box around the word* mariner *and writing the word below the passage. Let's see, I know the mariner is a man. He's dirty, has a beard, chews on a cigar, wears a sailor's cap, and has an anchor tattoo. Based on the sailor's hat and the tattoo of the anchor, I'm going to guess that the word* mariner *means "sailor" or "seaman."*

Then ask students to look up the word *mariner* in the dictionary to check your guess.

3. Let students work in pairs to figure out the meanings of the rest of the italicized words in the passage. Remind them to use the four steps. Discuss their responses and how the steps helped them determine the words' meanings.

Explain again how helpful context clues are. Although students won't be able to box words in books that they read, going over the steps mentally will enable them to see the context clues around unfamiliar words.

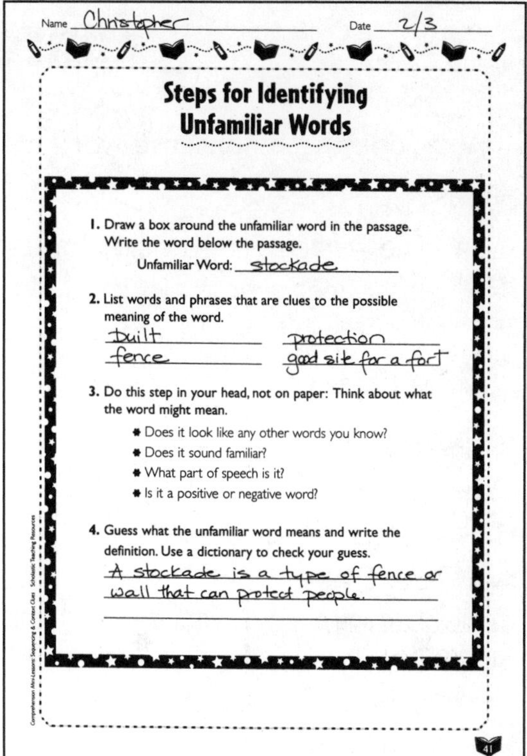

Name Christopher Date 2/3

Steps for Identifying Unfamiliar Words

1. Draw a box around the unfamiliar word in the passage. Write the word below the passage.
Unfamiliar Word: stockade

2. List words and phrases that are clues to the possible meaning of the word.
built protection
fence good site for a fort

3. Do this step in your head, not on paper: Think about what the word might mean.
- Does it look like any other words you know?
- Does it sound familiar?
- What part of speech is it?
- Is it a positive or negative word?

4. Guess what the unfamiliar word means and write the definition. Use a dictionary to check your guess.
A stockade is a type of fence or wall that can protect people.

41

Closing the Lesson

Use one or more of these activities to wrap up the mini-lesson.

- **Writing:** Challenge students to write two short paragraphs of one to three sentences about any topic. Have them replace one of the words in each paragraph with a nonsense word. Caution them to make sure to surround the nonsense word with enough context clues so that another student can figure out its meaning. They'll also use these passages with Mini-Lesson 2.

- **Assessment:** Ask students to write sentences using the words *mariner*, *sauntered*, and *musculature*.

Answers

Context Clues #1, page 40: *werbert*—sandwich; *locloey*—computer; *pytusul*—apples; *packrock*—elephant

Context Clues #2, page 42: *mariner*—a sailor (he wore a sailor's cap, had an anchor tattoo); *sauntered*—swaying walk (he walked "as if it was difficult for him to walk on solid ground"; "rolling walk"); *musculature*—build/muscular structure (he looked as if he was "used to hard, physical work"; "bulging arm muscles"; "ancient 'Popeye'")

Name ______________________ Date ______________

Context Clues #1

What does each nonsense word mean?

The *werbert* Sam brought for lunch looked delicious. It contained layers of roast beef, cheese, lettuce, and tomato piled in between two slices of bread. Sam couldn't wait to eat it.

Werbert means: ______________________

Clues: ______________________

____

The *locloey* is a very expensive but useful tool in the classroom. Students actually fight over whose turn it is to use it. Research, typing, games, and other activities can be done on it.

Locloey means: ______________________

Clues: ______________________

____

Tanya loved to pick *pytusul* in the fall. She would fill bushel baskets with the green or red fruit and use them to make pies, muffins, sauce, and other sweets.

Pytusul means: ______________________

Clues: ______________________

____

____

The *packrock* lives in both Asia and Africa. These enormous animals feast on foliage and use their long, prehensile trunks to drink water and pick up food. In parts of Asia and India, they are trained to work for humans. They carry loads and lift and move objects.

Packrock means: ______________________

Clues: ______________________

Name ______________________________ Date ______________

Steps for Identifying Unfamiliar Words

1. Draw a box around the unfamiliar word in the passage. Write the word below the passage.

Unfamiliar Word: ______________________

2. List words and phrases that are clues to the possible meaning of the word.

______________________ ______________________

______________________ ______________________

3. Do this step in your head, not on paper: Think about what the word might mean.

- Does it look like any other words you know?
- Does it sound familiar?
- What part of speech is it?
- Is it a positive or a negative word?

4. Guess what the unfamiliar word means and write the definition. Use a dictionary to check your guess.

____

____

____

Name ______________________ Date ______________

Context Clues #2

Use the four-step plan to figure out the meaning of the italicized words in the paragraph. Write the meaning and the clues that helped you.

The hunchbacked *mariner* had a long white beard like a goat's, a dirty, white sailor's cap on his head, a cigar stump in the corner of his mouth, and the tattoo of a ship's anchor on his arm. When he walked, he *sauntered* from side to side as if it was difficult for him to walk on solid ground. He had the *musculature* of someone who was used to hard, physical work. With his rolling walk and bulging arm muscles, the old man looked like an ancient "Popeye."

1. *mariner* means: ______________________

Clues: ______________________

____

____

2. *sauntered* means: ______________________

Clues: ______________________

____

____

3. *musculature* means: ______________________

Clues: ______________________

____

____

Context Clues Mini-Lesson 2

Context Clues Guidelines

Opening the Lesson

- I ask students to exchange the passages they wrote for Mini-Lesson 1 and figure out the meaning of the nonsense words using context clues.
- Then I have partners confirm each other's definitions.
- I set aside class time for my students to read aloud their passages—without revealing the nonsense words' definitions so the student audience has more opportunities to use context clues.

Teaching the Lesson

1. Hand out copies of the Context Clues Guidelines, and then display the transparency. Go over the guidelines and examples, making sure everyone understands them.
2. Create a pool of familiar vocabulary words that students can use in example sentences in the guidelines.

Idea

You can write the familiar vocabulary words on the chalkboard, create a transparency, or make a reproducible. I've found that giving my students a reproducible with the pool of vocabulary words is the most effective.

3. After pairing or grouping your students, ask them to use a vocabulary word in a sentence to exemplify each guideline.

Objective

Students apply context clues guidelines to help them define unfamiliar words.

Materials

student passages from Mini-Lesson 1, vocabulary words

Reproducibles

Context Clues Guidelines, page 45 (Make 1 copy for each student. Make 1 transparency.)

Context Clues Guideline Hunt, page 46 (Make 1 copy for each student.)

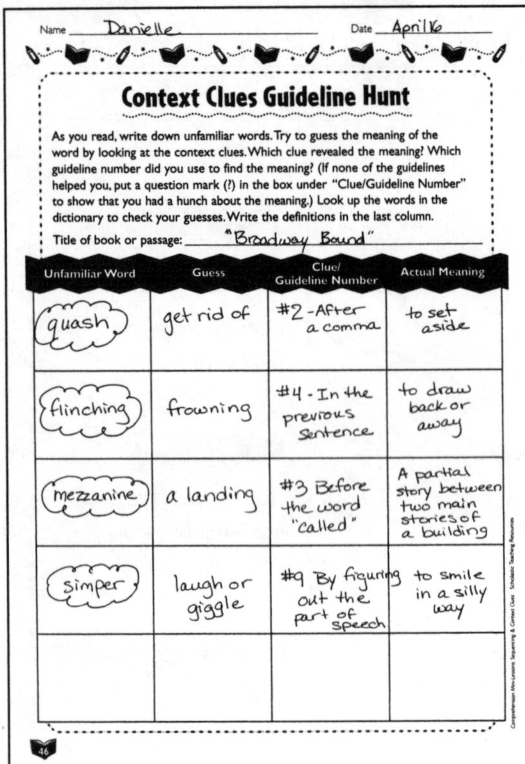

Name Danielle Date April 16

Context Clues Guideline Hunt

As you read, write down unfamiliar words. Try to guess the meaning of the word by looking at the context clues. Which clue revealed the meaning? Which guideline number did you use to find the meaning? (If none of the guidelines helped you, put a question mark (?) in the box under "Clue/Guideline Number" to show that you had a hunch about the meaning.) Look up the words in the dictionary to check your guesses. Write the definitions in the last column.

Title of book or passage: "Broadway Bound"

Unfamiliar Word	Guess	Clue/ Guideline Number	Actual Meaning
quash	get rid of	#2 - After a comma	to set aside
flinching	frowning	#4 - In the previous sentence	to draw back or away
mezzanine	a landing	#3 Before the word "called"	A partial story between two main stories of a building
simper	laugh or giggle	#9 By figuring out the part of speech	to smile in a silly way

Comprehension Mini-Lessons: Sequencing & Context Clues Scholastic Teaching Resources

46

Closing the Lesson

Use one or more of these activities to wrap up the mini-lesson.

- **Assessment:** Assign passages from textbooks for students to read. Ask them to fill out the Context Clues Guideline Hunt as they read. This reproducible gives students the opportunity to see examples within actual text.
- **Journal:** Ask students to write about which guidelines have been the most effective in helping them use context clues.

Name ______________________ Date ______________

Context Clues Guidelines

Look for clues to the meanings of words—

1. after the word or that directly follow the unfamiliar word.
Example: The trek, or journey, became more challenging as we approached the top of the mountain.

2. after a comma that directly follows the word.
Example: In order to keep the dogs inside our yard, we built a parapet, a low wall or railing.

3. before the word *called*.
Example: The worm ate the middle layer of the peach, which is called the mesocarp.

4. in the previous sentence.
Example: Everyone at the dinner table cleaned their plates and asked for seconds. As the guests left, they said the dinner was delectable.

5. in the next sentence.
Example: Jake left the waitress a paltry tip. She forgot to give them glasses of water, brought out cold food, and never checked on them, so she deserved a small tip.

6. by replacing the unfamiliar word with a "prediction" word to see if it fits or makes sense.
Example: He acted like a buffoon at the party by telling jokes and laughing too loudly and too often.
(prediction word: *fool*)

7. by studying the unfamiliar word's prefix, suffix, or root word and writing the meanings to figure out the meaning of the word.
Example: The only part of the city recognizable to Ian was the Sears Tower.
(-able = capable of being/recognizable = capable of being recognized)

8. by asking yourself if the word sounds positive or negative.
Example: The evil queen cast a sinister glare at the elf when he asked her a question. (evil = negative)

9. by figuring out the word's part of speech, such as a noun, verb, adjective, or adverb.
Example: He guzzled water rapidly after the race.
(*Guzzled* is a verb. He did something to the water.)

Name ______________________ Date ______________

Context Clues Guideline Hunt

As you read, write down unfamiliar words. Try to guess the meaning of the word by looking at the context clues. Which clue revealed the meaning? Which guideline number did you use to find the meaning? (If none of the guidelines helped you, put a question mark (?) in the box under "Clue/Guideline Number" to show that you had a hunch about the meaning.) Look up the words in the dictionary to check your guesses. Write the definitions in the last column.

Title of book or passage: ______________________

Unfamiliar Word	Guess	Clue/ Guideline Number	Actual Meaning

Comprehension Mini-Lessons: Sequencing & Context Clues Scholastic Teaching Resources

Context Clues Mini-Lesson 3

Figuring It Out

Opening the Lesson

* I use this activity to show the power of context clues to my students. I display one section from the Add On transparency and follow these guidelines as I read each line in order:

  - Reveal the first line (the unfamiliar word). Cover the rest of the lines with blank paper.
  - Ask students to identify the meaning of the word. If a student knows the meaning at this point, I ask him or her to whisper it to me instead of telling the whole class.
  - Reveal the next line (two words).
  - Ask students again to identify the meaning of the word. If they can't, I ask if they now have a small clue (perhaps the part of speech).
  - Continue to reveal each line, and ask students the meaning of the unfamiliar word. They must justify their predictions.
  - When the whole sentence has been revealed and students have made their guesses, show them the answer (final line).

Tip

I sometimes ask my students to write their guesses after each line is revealed and read. In this way, students who quickly figure out the meaning of the word can take satisfaction in recording their answer, but will not ruin it for the rest of the class.

  - We talk about how each clue helped them guess the meaning. I emphasize that when they come across an unfamiliar word in their reading they may have to look for several context clues and not just one.

Teaching the Lesson

1. Let your students practice using context clues in an authentic situation. Have a variety of books or magazines on hand for them to choose from.

Objective

Students document the steps they use to figure out the meanings of unfamiliar words in a passage.

Materials

a variety of on-level books or classroom magazines, dictionary

Reproducibles

Add On, page 49 (Make 1 transparency for each section of the page or cut the transparency into three parts.)

Figuring It Out, page 50 (Make 1 copy for each student.)

2. As they read, they'll be filling out the Figuring It Out reproducible. Pass out the reproducible and discuss it. Any unfamiliar words go in the first column. Then they should look for context clues around the word. Remind students that these clues could be a whole paragraph before or after the unknown word. Whatever clues they find (prefix, suffix, root, part of speech, and so on) go in the second column. Based on these clues, your students should guess the meaning of the word and write it in the third column. Finally, have them look up the definition in the dictionary to confirm their guesses. They should write this definition in the fourth column. If their guess was correct, tell them to write a plus sign in the last column. If their guess was incorrect, they should write a minus sign. Emphasize that it doesn't matter if their guesses were incorrect; the aim is for you to see how close they came to guessing the correct definition.

3. Allow plenty of silent reading time for this activity.

Closing the Lesson

Use one or more of these activities to wrap up the mini-lesson.

- **Journal:** Encourage students to write a paragraph about their feelings during the Figuring It Out activity. Did they ever get frustrated? Why did they feel that way? Did they ever feel successful or surprised? Discuss these feelings in class. Share the fact that you and other adults still encounter unfamiliar words—and sometimes there aren't any context clues. Ask students what they could do in that situation.

- **Assessment:** Challenge your students to create their own Add-On section for an unfamiliar word. Then let them play the role of the teacher and reveal the lines one by one until another student guesses the correct meaning.

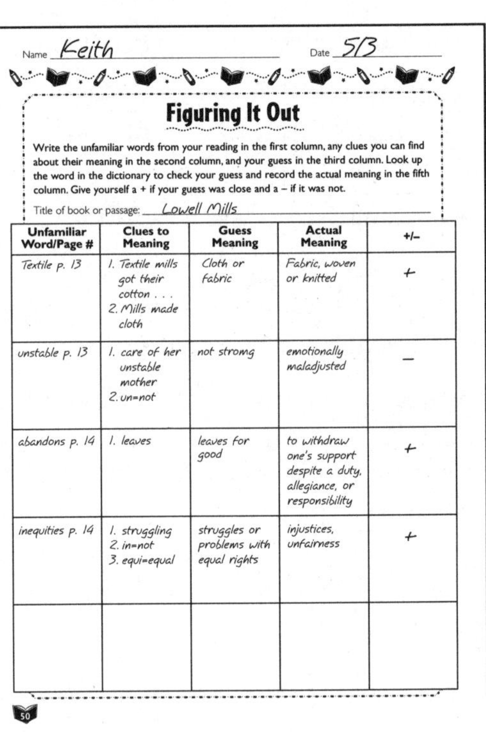

Name *Keith* Date *5/3*

Figuring It Out

Write the unfamiliar words from your reading in the first column, any clues you can find about their meaning in the second column, and your guess in the third column. Look up the word in the dictionary to check your guess and record the actual meaning in the fifth column. Give yourself a + if your guess was close and a – if it was not.

Title of book or passage: *Lowell Mills*

Unfamiliar Word/Page #	Clues to Meaning	Guess Meaning	Actual Meaning	+/–
Textile p. 13	*1. Textile mills got their cotton . . . 2. Mills made cloth*	*Cloth or fabric*	*Fabric, woven or knitted*	+
unstable p. 13	*1. care of her unstable mother 2. un=not*	*not stromg*	*emotionally maladjusted*	–
abandons p. 14	*1. leaves*	*leaves for good*	*to withdraw one's support despite a duty, allegiance, or responsibility*	+
inequities p. 14	*1. struggling 2. in=not 3. equi=equal*	*struggles or problems with equal rights*	*injustices, unfairness*	+

50

Add On

The norpul ________________

The little norpul ________________

The little norpul crawled ________________

The little norpul crawled across ________________

The little norpul crawled across the limb ________________

The little norpul crawled across the limb with the nut. ________________

ANSWER: **squirrel**

edifice

The tall edifice ________________

The tall edifice added ________________

The tall edifice added beauty ________________

The tall edifice added beauty to the city ________________

The tall edifice added beauty to the city after three years ________________

The tall edifice added beauty to the city after three years of construction. ________________

ANSWER: **building or skyscraper**

callow

The callow ________________

The callow baby-sitter ________________

The callow baby-sitter jumped ________________

The callow baby-sitter jumped on the couch ________________

The callow baby-sitter jumped on the couch and stuck out her tongue ________________

The callow baby-sitter jumped on the couch and stuck out her tongue at the crying child. ________________

ANSWER: **immature or inexperienced**

Name ______________________________ Date ______________

Figuring It Out

Write the unfamiliar words from your reading in the first column, any clues you can find about their meaning in the second column, and your guess in the third column. Look up the word in the dictionary to check your guess and record the actual meaning in the fifth column. Give yourself a + if your guess was close and a – if it was not.

Title of book or passage: ______________________________

Unfamiliar Word/Page #	Clues to Meaning	Guess Meaning	Actual Meaning	+/–

Comprehension Mini-Lessons: Sequencing & Context Clues Scholastic Teaching Resources

Context Clues Mini-Lesson 4

Affixes and Roots

Opening the Lesson

- I write the words *benediction* and *geothermal* on the chalkboard and ask my students to write down guesses about their meanings. Since there are no context clues around the words, they must study the words to try to figure out their meanings.
- During our discussion of the words, I explain that by looking at the parts of words, we can figure out their meanings. Words are often formed by placing affixes—prefixes and suffixes—and root words together. Then I share the following examples:

  Benediction means "a speech of well being."
  clues within word: *bene* = well; *diction* = speech

  Geothermal means "heat of the earth."
  clues within word: *geo* = earth; *thermal* = heat

Teaching the Lesson

1. Knowing the meanings of common affixes and roots can help students quickly figure out the meanings of unfamiliar words—especially when the words don't have a context. It takes time and effort to learn and remember these affixes and roots, but your class should be able to learn about 50 of them within two weeks.
2. Look through the list of Common Affixes and Roots, and choose the ones that you feel are the most important for students to know. This activity calls for two or three affixes or roots per student, so if you have a class of 20 students, choose a total of 40 to 60 affixes and roots.
3. Make a copy of the Common Affixes and Roots reproducible. Cut out the affixes and roots you want to use. Fold the strips and place them in a container so each student may draw two or three strips.
4. Then distribute two or three copies of the My Research Web reproducible to each student. Explain that they will use this web to research their affixes or roots so they will become experts on these word parts. Make sure everyone understands how to fill in the reproducible.

Objective

Students complete a web for affixes or roots.

Materials

50 three- by five-inch index cards for each student

Reproducibles

Common Affixes and Roots, pages 53–55 (Make 1 copy.)

My Research Web, page 56 (Make 2 or 3 copies for each student.)

5. When students have turned in their webs, assign the role of teacher to two or three students each day. Their job will be to use their research webs to teach their affix or root to the class. Emphasize how important it is for each student to see the Picture Memory Clue on the web. While a student is teaching, the other students will take notes on index cards. These cards will become their flashcards for learning the affixes or roots. A sample card appears below.

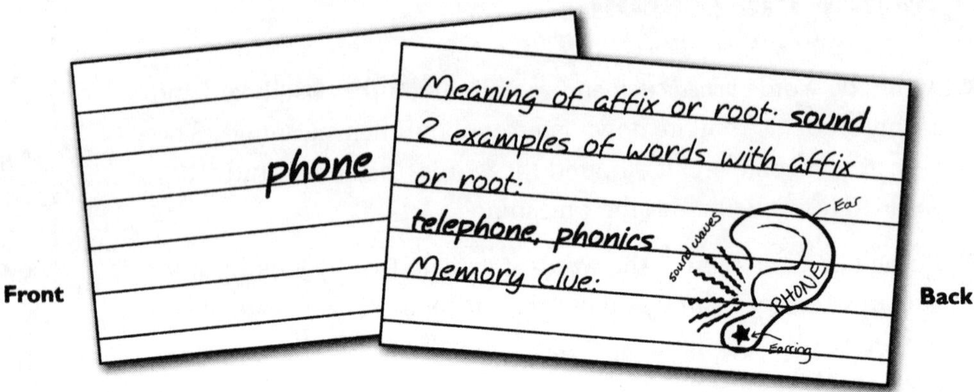

Closing the Lesson

Use one or more of these activities to wrap up the mini-lesson.

- **Review:** In order to make sure students remember these affixes or roots, set aside time each day so that partners can review them. Make a large chart of the affixes and roots you've studied. Leave plenty of room for students to fill in new words they find that contain these affixes or roots from their class or independent reading. Encourage them to write a short definition that shows how the word is related to the affix or root.
- **Homework:** Have students take their flashcards home to learn the terms.
- **Assessment:** Students will remember the information better if you give them several quizzes rather than one comprehensive test. To reinforce my students' learning, I quiz them daily about the affixes and roots they've learned up to that point.

Name ______________________ Date ______________

Common Affixes and Roots

ab = away abduct = carry away (verb) abnormal = away from normal (adj.)	capit = head capital = head city (n.) decapitate = cut off the head (v.)
an = without anarchy = without a chief (n.) anaerobic = without oxygen (adj.)	cide = kill suicide = killing of oneself (n.) insecticide = killing of insects (n.)
ante = before antebellum = before the Civil War (adj.) antedate = come before in time (v.)	circum = together circumference = measure around a circle (n.) circumvent = surround (v.)
anti = against antiseptic = against decay (adj.) antislavery = against slavery (adj.)	col = together collect = gather together (v.) colony = group living together (n.)
anthrop = human being anthropology = study of humans (n.) philanthropist = lover of humans (n.)	com = together combine = put together (v.) compact = squeezed together (adj.)
aqua = water aquarium = container that holds water and fish (n.) aquatic = relating to water (adj.)	con = together congregate = group together (v.) converge = come together (v.)
auto = self autobiography = self-written life story (n.) automatic = operating by itself (adj.)	contra = against contradict = speak against something (v.) contrary = against something (adj.)
arch = chief archenemy = chief enemy (n.) architect = chief builder (n.)	cosmo = world cosmography = description of world (n.) cosmopolitan = relating to the whole world (adj.)
astron = star astronomy = study of stars (n.) astronaut = traveler around stars (n.)	crat = rule democrat = one who believes that people rule (n.) autocrat = one who believes in self-rule (n.)
bene = well benefit = do well for (v.) benevolent = treating well (adj.)	de = from degrade = take worth from (v.) defile = take purity from (v.)
bi = two bicycle = two-wheel cycle (n.) bigamy = practice of having two spouses (n.)	dict = say diction = the way something is said (n.) dictator = leader who has only say (n.)
bio = life biology = study of life (n.) biography = written life story (n.)	dynam = power dynamite = powerful destroyer (n.) dynasty = powerful family (n.)

Name ______________________ Date ______________

Common Affixes and Roots

extra = beyond extravagant = beyond the budget (adj.) extraordinary = beyond ordinary (adj.)	iso = equal isogonic = having equal angles (adj.) isothermal = having equal temperatures (adj.)
ex = out expire = breathe out (v.) extinguish = put out (v.)	ject = throw reject = throw away (v.) projectile = something that is thrown (n.)
frater = brother fraternize = act as brothers (v.) fraternity = brotherhood (n.)	macro = large macrocosm = the universe (n.) macrobiotic = promoting long life through diet (adj.)
ge *or* geo = earth geography = study of places on earth (n.) geology = study of earth's elements (n.)	manu = hand manuscript = handwriting (n.) manually = by hand (adj.)
graph = write graphology = study of handwriting (n.) autograph = self-written name (n.)	mand = order mandate = an order (n.) mandatory = commanded (adj.)
greg = group congregate = group together (v.) gregarious = taking pleasure in being in a group (adj.)	mater = mother maternity = motherhood (n.) matriarch = woman who rules family (n.)
gress = move progress = move forward (v.) aggressive = moving toward (adj.)	med = middle medium = in the middle (adj.) mediator = person who acts in the middle (n.)
hemi = half hemisphere = half of the world (n.) hemiplegic = half-paralyzed (adj.)	meter = measure thermometer = measure of heat (n.) speedometer = measure of speed (n.)
homo = same homogenized = the same throughout (adj.) homographs = words written the same (n.)	micro = small microcosm = small world (n.) microsecond = one-millionth of a second (n.)
hydra = water hydrant = discharge pipe for water (n.) dehydrate = remove water from (v.)	mis = wrong misbehave = use wrong behavior (v.) misprint = wrong printing (n.)
inter = between intervene = come between (v.) intercity = between cities (adj.)	mono = one monogamy = practice of having one spouse (n.) monologue = speech by one person (n.)
inter = within interior = within the inside (adj.) internal = on the inside (adj.)	onym = name homonym = same name (n.) autonym = opposite name (n.)

Name ______________________ Date ____________

Common Affixes and Roots

ob = against object = speak against (v.) obstacle = something going against progress (n.)	psych = mind psychiatry = healing of the mind (n.) psyche = mind or soul (n.)
pan = all panacea = cure-all (n.) pandemic = affecting all things (adj.)	pre = before preview = see before (v.) prediction = something said before (n.)
pater = father paternity = fatherhood (n.) paternal = fatherly (adj.)	re = again return = go back again (v.) reunite = unite again (v.)
peri = around perimeter = measurement around (n.) periphery = the edge around (n.)	scope = see telescope = device used to see far off (n.) periscope = device used to see around (n.)
per = through permeate = soak through (v.) perforate = put holes through (v.)	se = apart secluded = set apart (adj.) secede = move apart from something (v.)
philo = love philosophy = love of wisdom (n.) audiophile = lover of sound (n.)	sed = remain sedentary = remaining in one place (adj.) sedative = drug which causes a person to remain calm (n.)
phone = sound phonics = system of learning by sound (n.) microphone = instrument that enlarges sound (n.)	semi = half semi-retired = half-retired (adj.) semi-circle = half-circle (n.)
poly = many polytheism = belief in many gods (n.) monopoly = many owned by one (n.)	oph = wise sophisticated = worldly wise (adj.) philosophy = love of wisdom (n.)
port = carry transport = carry across (v.) portable = able to be carried (adj.)	tele = far off television = device that transmits pictures from far off (n.) telephone = device that transmits sound from far off (n.)
post = after postpone = change date to later time (v.) posthumous = after death (adj.)	theo = God theology = study of God (n.) theism = belief in God (n.)
pro = before prophecy = knowledge before of what will happen (n.) propose = to set before (v.)	thermo = heat thermodynamics = power of heat (n.) thermos = container that keeps in liquid heat (n.)
pseudo = false pseudonym = false name (n.) pseudoscience = false science (n.)	vid = see video = visual aspect of TV (n.) visual = able to be seen (adj.)

Name ______________________ Date ______________

MY RESEARCH WEB: Affixes and Roots

MEANING:

AFFIX or ROOT: ______________

PICTURE MEMORY CLUE:

EXAMPLES:

1. Word: ______________

Definition: ______________

Sentence: ______________

2. Word: ______________

Definition: ______________

Sentence: ______________

3. Word: ______________

Definition: ______________

Sentence: ______________

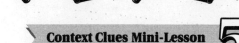

Test-Taking Format

Opening the Lesson

- To help my students review context clues, I create a quiz with six or seven vocabulary words they've recently learned. Ideally, the quiz should be tied to a unit the class has just studied.
- The American Revolution Summary Quiz shows a quiz I created for my fifth-grade students. Notice the Word Bank at the bottom of the page. If this quiz fits your curriculum, feel free to use it. If not, you can use it as a template to create your own curriculum-appropriate quiz.

Teaching the Lesson

1. Tell students that on standardized tests they will have to figure out the meaning of words in passages. They will need to read the entire passage in order to determine the meaning of the word. In other words, they'll be looking for clues within the context of the passage.
2. To familiarize students with context-clue work in a test-taking format, distribute copies of the Mosquitoes and West Nile Virus passage. Place the transparency on the overhead projector, and read it aloud as a class. Then pair students, and have them use their copies of the Context Clues Guidelines Sheet from Mini-Lesson 2 to help them figure out the answers to the questions about the words in the passage. Assure them that there are several clues within the text that will help them out. Discuss your students' responses and how the Context Clues Guidelines helped them determine the words' meanings.
3. Let students work independently to complete the Tetra's Role in Science passage. Check these answers in class, and discuss the clues within the text.

Objective

Students choose the correct meaning for unfamiliar words in standardized test passages.

Materials

teacher-created quiz; cloze set passage from content-area reading book

Reproducibles

Context Clues Guidelines Sheet, page 45

American Revolution Summary Quiz (or other curriculum-appropriate quiz), page 59 (Make 1 copy for each student.)

Mosquitoes and West Nile Virus, page 60 (Make 1 copy for each student. Make 1 transparency.)

Tetra's Role in Science, page 61 (Make 1 copy for each student.)

Closing the Lesson

Use one or more of these activities to wrap up the mini-lesson.

- **Assessment:** Choose a passage from a content-area reading book for students to read. Create multiple-choice questions for unfamiliar or difficult words in the passage, and have students answer them. These passages usually contain great examples of context clues.
- **Journal:** Challenge students to record unfamiliar words they encounter in their reading and also how they figured out their meanings. Encourage them to make this an ongoing activity. Writing down the words and the strategies used to uncover meaning is a great way to reinforce learning.

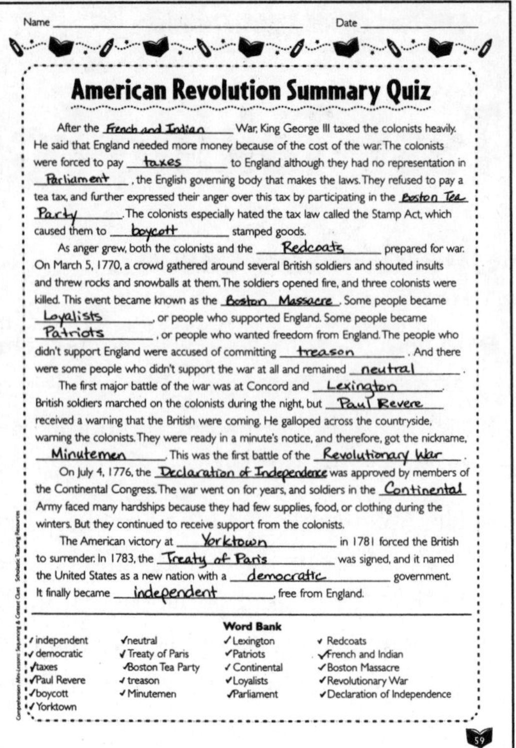

Name ____________ Date ____________

American Revolution Summary Quiz

After the French and Indian War, King George III taxed the colonists heavily. He said that England needed more money because of the cost of the war. The colonists were forced to pay taxes to England although they had no representation in Parliament, the English governing body that makes the laws. They refused to pay a tea tax, and further expressed their anger over this tax by participating in the Boston Tea Party. The colonists especially hated the tax law called the Stamp Act, which caused them to boycott stamped goods.

As anger grew, both the colonists and the Redcoats prepared for war. On March 5, 1770, a crowd gathered around several British soldiers and shouted insults and threw rocks and snowballs at them. The soldiers opened fire, and three colonists were killed. This event became known as the Boston Massacre. Some people became Loyalists, or people who supported England. Some people became Patriots, or people who wanted freedom from England. The people who didn't support England were accused of committing treason. And there were some people who didn't support the war at all and remained neutral.

The first major battle of the war was at Concord and Lexington. British soldiers marched on the colonists during the night, but Paul Revere received a warning that the British were coming. He galloped across the countryside, warning the colonists. They were ready in a minute's notice, and therefore, got the nickname, Minutemen. This was the first battle of the Revolutionary War.

On July 4, 1776, the Declaration of Independence was approved by members of the Continental Congress. The war went on for years, and soldiers in the Continental Army faced many hardships because they had few supplies, food, or clothing during the winters. But they continued to receive support from the colonists.

The American victory at Yorktown in 1781 forced the British to surrender. In 1783, the Treaty of Paris was signed, and it named the United States as a new nation with a democratic government. It finally became independent, free from England.

Word Bank

✓independent	✓neutral	✓Lexington	✓Redcoats
✓democratic	✓Treaty of Paris	✓Patriots	✓French and Indian
✓taxes	✓Boston Tea Party	✓Continental	✓Boston Massacre
✓Paul Revere	✓treason	✓Loyalists	✓Revolutionary War
✓boycott	✓Minutemen	✓Parliament	✓Declaration of Independence
✓Yorktown			

59

Answers

Mosquitoes and West Nile Virus, page 60: 1. A; 2. A; 3. C

Tetra's Role in Science, page 61: 1. D; 2. D; 3. D

Name ______________________________ Date ______________

American Revolution Summary Quiz

After the ______________________ War, King George III taxed the colonists heavily. He said that England needed more money because of the cost of the war. The colonists were forced to pay ________________ to England although they had no representation in ________________ , the English governing body that makes the laws. They refused to pay a tea tax, and further expressed their anger over this tax by participating in the ____________ ______________. The colonists especially hated the tax law called the Stamp Act, which caused them to ____________________ stamped goods.

As anger grew, both the colonists and the ____________________ prepared for war. On March 5, 1770, a crowd gathered around several British soldiers and shouted insults and threw rocks and snowballs at them. The soldiers opened fire, and three colonists were killed. This event became known as the ____________________. Some people became ____________________, or people who supported England. Some people became ____________________ , or people who wanted freedom from England. The people who didn't support England were accused of committing ____________________ . And there were some people who didn't support the war at all and remained __________________ .

The first major battle of the war was at Concord and ____________________. British soldiers marched on the colonists during the night, but ____________________ received a warning that the British were coming. He galloped across the countryside, warning the colonists. They were ready on a minute's notice, and therefore, got the nickname, ______________________. This was the first battle of the ______________________ .

On July 4, 1776, the ____________________________ was approved by members of the Continental Congress. The war went on for years, and soldiers in the ______________ Army faced many hardships because they had few supplies, food, or clothing during the winters. But they continued to receive support from the colonists.

The American victory at __________________________ in 1781 forced the British to surrender. In 1783, the ____________________________ was signed, and it named the United States as a new nation with a ____________________________ government. It finally became __________________________, free from England.

Word Bank

independent	neutral	Lexington	Redcoats
democratic	Treaty of Paris	Patriots	French and Indian
taxes	Boston Tea Party	Continental	Boston Massacre
Paul Revere	treason	Loyalists	Revolutionary War
boycott	Minutemen	Parliament	Declaration of Independence
Yorktown			

Name ______________________ Date ______________

Mosquitoes and West Nile Virus

Mosquito bites are not just itchy irritations anymore. Now they're causing severe illness and, in some cases, death.

Experts believe some mosquitoes carry a strain of the West Nile virus, which causes encephalitis, or swelling of the brain. Encephalitis symptoms include fever and a headache. In the most severe cases, victims fall into a coma.

The mosquitoes become infected by feeding on birds that have the virus. The mosquitoes then transmit, or pass, the virus to humans and animals.

Scientists had never before found the West Nile strain of the virus in the United States, and the search continues to find out how the virus got to this country. It could have been in the blood of a foreign visitor or of a bird that had flown here from another country.

In an effort to kill virus-carrying mosquitoes, areas of the country such as New York, Connecticut, and New Jersey have been sprayed with pesticides. But experts worry that the virus will spread as migrating birds continue to carry the virus around the country.

So far, there is no cure or vaccine for the virus. Experts say that very young children and the elderly are at the greatest risk. What's the best way to protect yourself from mosquitoes? Wear long-sleeved shirts and long pants, and spray yourself with insect repellent.

Choose the best answer.

1. What is the meaning of the word *severe*?

(A) serious
(B) slight
(C) heavy
(D) loud

2. In this passage, the word *transmit* means—

(A) to pass
(B) to travel
(C) to search
(D) to receive

3. An insect *repellent* is something that—

(A) encourages insects to breed
(B) causes people to get sick
(C) keeps away insects
(D) spreads disease

Comprehension Mini-Lessons: Sequencing & Context Clues Scholastic Teaching Resources

Name ______________________ Date ______________

Tetra's Role in Science

Tetra, a rhesus monkey, would never be mistaken for a doctor. But scientists in Beaverton, Oregon, hope he can help them find the cure for human illnesses such as cancer, diabetes, and heart disease.

The one-month-old Tetra is a clone, a living thing artificially created by scientists to have the same genes as another animal. Genes are the parts of living cells that are passed from parents to children. Genes determine how people, animals, and plants look and grow.

Scientists created Tetra by re-creating the way identical twins are born. Although human identical twins are born often, monkeys rarely give birth to identical twins. Scientists divided one embryo, or a living thing at its earliest stage of growth, into two embryos. They implanted each embryo into a different monkey mommy.

Studying identical monkeys—whose genes resemble human genes—could give researchers clues about how to stop human diseases.

Choose the best answer.

1. What is a *clone*?

Ⓐ It determines how living things look and grow.
Ⓑ It causes human diseases such as cancer.
Ⓒ It is passed from parents to children.
Ⓓ It is an artificially created living thing.

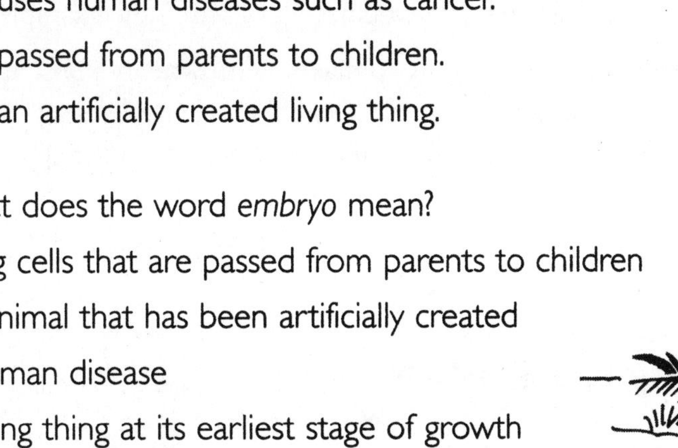

2. What does the word *embryo* mean?

Ⓐ living cells that are passed from parents to children
Ⓑ an animal that has been artificially created
Ⓒ a human disease
Ⓓ a living thing at its earliest stage of growth

3. In this passage, what does the word *identical* mean?

Ⓐ different
Ⓑ living
Ⓒ earliest
Ⓓ same

Objective

Students create a No-Nonsense Book that uses context clues to help define made-up words.

Duration

1–2 weeks (Plan to do this project after you teach a unit.)

Materials

list of 10 vocabulary words, social studies or science textbook, 13 sheets of white or light-colored construction paper (for each student), markers, stapler and staples, blank transparency (optional)

Reproducibles

Student Project Sheet, page 63 (Make 1 copy for each student. Make 1 transparency.)

Putting It All Together: No-Nonsense Books

Preparing for the Project

- Make a list of 10 vocabulary words from a chapter or unit you have just completed in a curriculum area such as social studies or science. Duplicate copies for your students. Then create a nonsense word example page to write on the board or a blank transparency. This is one I created for a science unit. The answer is *biome*. Be sure to include some strong context clues.

> **#1**
> There are six major jolotties in the world. Each one of these jolotties received its name because of its climate and weather. In Ohio, we live in the deciduous forest jolottie.
> Answer: ______________________

Introducing the Project

1. Display your nonsense word example page, and explain that you have substituted a nonsense word for a real word. Remind students that the real word is one they just studied. When they have guessed what the real word is, discuss the context clues you used in the example.
2. Tell students that they're going to make their own No-Nonsense books based on vocabulary words they've learned recently. Pass out the Student Project Sheet. Go over the steps, and make sure everyone understands how to do the project.
3. Let students work on their booklets until they've used all the vocabulary words.

Assessing the Project

- **Students Working Together:** Have students exchange completed No-Nonsense Books and guess the real words. They should check the answer key to verify their answers and give feedback to the author on how well the clues were written.
- **Verbal:** Ask students to share the process they used to create one of their nonsense words.

Name ______________________________ Date ____________________

No-Nonsense Book

Student Project Sheet

Follow the steps below to create a No-Nonsense Book.

1. Staple the pages of your No-Nonsense Book together. Here's what the pages should contain.

- **Cover page:** Write the title, No-Nonsense Book, and the title of the chapter or unit the vocabulary words are from. Also write your name and the date.
- **Pages 1–10:** Write one or more sentences full of context clues for each vocabulary word on the list. Then make up a silly nonsense word like *zeemee* or *clonclon* to replace the vocabulary word. Underline the word. Put one word on each page.

> **1.**
> Because supplies were limited during World War II, sugar and meat were zambidoes to American households.
>
> Answer: ______________________________

- **Answer Key, page 11:** Write the answers on this page.
- **Reader Feedback, page 12:** You'll exchange No-Nonsense Books with a partner. After guessing the meaning of each nonsense word and checking the answer key, they'll give you feedback about how easy or difficult your clues were. Leave space for two compliments and one suggestion.

> **Answer Key for No-Nonsense Book**
>
> 1. zambidoes—rationed

> **Reader Feedback**
>
> Compliments:
>
> 1. ______________________________
>
> 2. ______________________________
>
> Suggestion for change:
>
> ______________________________

Teacher Resources

Beech, Linda Ward. *Ready-to-Go Reproducibles: Short Reading Passages and Graphic Organizers to Build Comprehension (Grades 4–5* and *Grades 6–8).* New York: Scholastic, Inc. 2001.

Billmeyer, Rachel and Mary Lee Barton. *Teaching Reading in the Content Areas: If Not Me, Then Who?* Aurora, CO: McREL, 1998.

Bixby, M. *Prove It: Whole Language Strategies for Secondary Students.* Katonah, NY: Richard Owen Publishing Co., 1988.

Howard, Mary. *Helping Your Struggling Students Be More Successful Readers (Grades 4–6)* Tulsa, OK: Reading Connections, 2003.*

Robb, Laura. *Reading Strategies That Work.* New York: Scholastic, Inc. 1995.

Wilhelm, Jeffrey D. *Action Strategies for Deepening Comprehension.* New York: Scholastic, Inc. 2002.

Wilhelm, Jeffrey D. *Improving Comprehension With Think-Aloud Strategies.* New York: Scholastic, Inc. 2001.

* This book is available at *http://wwwdrmaryhoward.com.*